Out to Lunch™

A Brand New

TRIBUNE
PUBLISHING
Orlando/1993

OUT TO LUNCH™
A BRAND NEW SHOE®

A publication of Tribune Publishing
and Tribune Media Services, Inc.

For information:
Tribune Publishing
P.O. Box 1100, Orlando, Florida 32802

Printed in the United States
First edition: January 1993
Second edition: May 1993

ISBN 0-941263-67-3

DEDICATION

To Susie,
the real Roz,
with love.

INTRODUCTION

In the early *Shoe* strips, Roz's roost was a bird feeder. Business was brisk, the birds became more human, and soon we had to hack out a big chunk of a huge oak tree to make room for a bigger counter.

Whether you are a bird or a human, the creature that feeds you is a very important part of your life. Roz quickly became a key character in the strip, and Roz's roost the setting for just about every philosophical discussion that has ever taken place in *Shoe.*

Roz is part waitress, part wise-mouthed bartender, and part mom. She presides over a combination fast-food place, saloon, back porch and kitchen table.

Like so many places like hers, Roz's roost owes its prosperity to the mixed blessing of being within stumbling distance of a newsroom – in her case, *The Treetops Tattler-Tribune.*

While I was based in Chicago, there was always "The Goat" or Ricardo's; back in Chapel Hill we had the Dairy Bar next door; and in Richmond it was Tom's and then Perly's (try the Bud MacNelly sandwich – it was named for my Dad...). We all have these special places in our lives. I hope you'll recognize yours at Roz's.

Enjoy.

– Jeff MacNelly

PATÉ? WHAT THE HECK IS PATÉ?
WELL, BASICALLY PATÉ IS A CHOPPED MEAT PRODUCT... BUT I CAN'T THINK OF THE RIGHT WORD FOR IT...
HOW 'BOUT "SPAM"?
MENU
MENU
MENU
MACNELLY

1

LOOK, SHOE! MY FAVORITE!

CREAM OF LEFTOVER.
MACNELLY

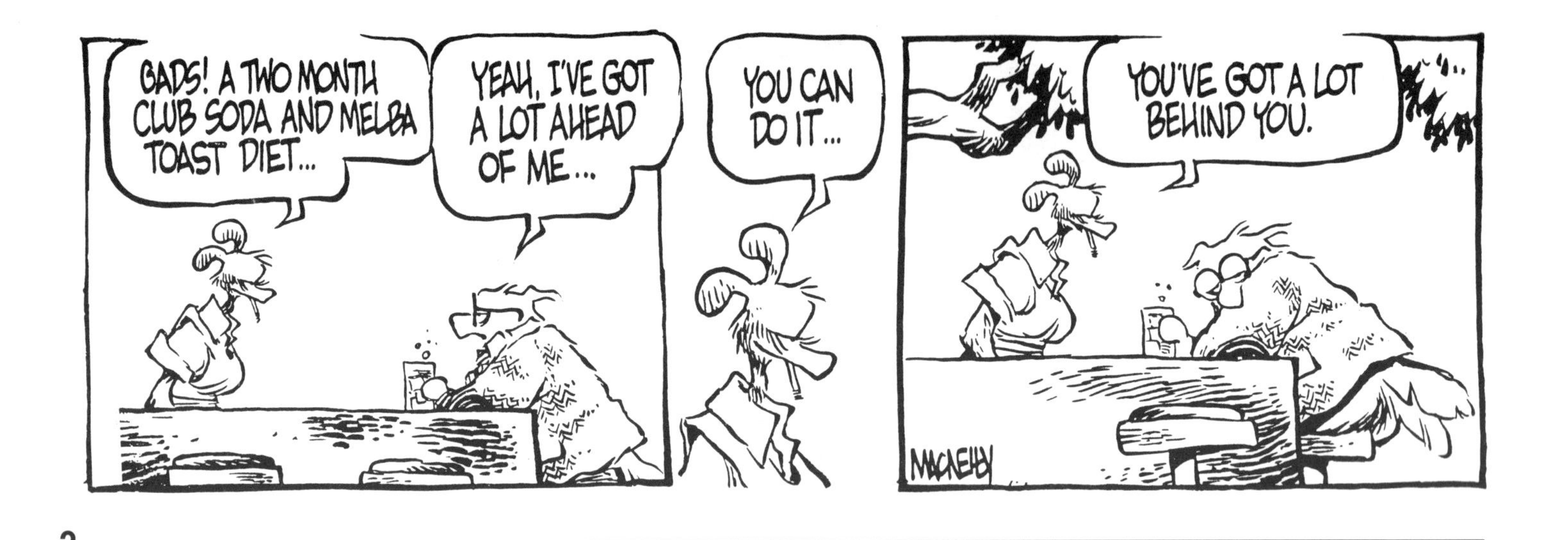
GADS! A TWO MONTH CLUB SODA AND MELBA TOAST DIET...
YEAH, I'VE GOT A LOT AHEAD OF ME...
YOU CAN DO IT...
YOU'VE GOT A LOT BEHIND YOU.
MACNELLY

YOU WANNA TRY A DIET THAT WILL REALLY WORK?
SURE!
IT'S MY PATENTED WEIGHT-LOSS METHOD FOR SENIOR CITIZENS.
JUST USE YOUR POLI-GRIP ON THE BUSINESS END OF YOUR DENTURES.
MACNELLY

Shoe
BY JEFF MACNELLY
WHAT'S ON?
AN ANCIENT FRENCH DISH...

AN OLD BRIGITTE BARDOT FLICK?

OH, GREAT!! I LOVE THESE COOKING SHOWS!
AND, WOW, THAT SURE DOES LOOK DELICIOUS!
AND WHAT A GREAT PICTURE!!

YOU CAN ALMOST SMELL THAT STUFF COOKING!!

3

WHAT'S THIS I'M WATCHING, ANYWAY?

MEAT LOAF.

YOU'RE WATCHING MY MICROWAVE.
MACNELLY

WHADDYA HAVE BESIDES THE POTATO SOUP?
WE HAVE THE SOUP DU JOUR-VICHYSSOISE.
WHAT'S THAT?
COLD POTATO SOUP.
MENU
MACNELLY

MAY I SUGGEST A BOTTLE OF BORDEAUX WITH THAT?
SURE.
IT COMPLEMENTS THE MEAT LOAF.
AND THIS MEAT LOAF CAN USE ALL THE COMPLIMENTS IT CAN GET.
MACNELLY

I DON'T SEE WHAT YOU CAN LIKE ABOUT SMOKING CIGARS...
NAME ONE THING THAT NASTY CIGAR IS GOOD FOR.
CROWD CONTROL.
MACNELLY

THIS TIME I'M GOING TO COMPLIMENT ROZ ON HER COOKING NO MATTER HOW NASTY IT TASTES...

MMM!! ROZ, THIS STEAK IS FANTASTIC!!
KLONG

IT'S LIVER, TOADFACE...
MACNELLY

BY JEFF MACNELLY
MORNIN', ROZ!! I'LL HAVE HALF A GRAPEFRUIT...

WHICH HALF?
GADS!! YOU KNOW I HATE THESE DECISIONS THIS EARLY IN THE MORNING...

GUSH!!

BLIT

GLICK

CHOMP
CHOMBLE

BLURT!

SQUEEZE
DRIBBLE

SLURP!

DELIGHTFUL GRAPEFRUIT, ROZ.
MACNELLY

WHAT KIND OF DRESSING YOU WANT ON YOUR SALAD? FRENCH, ITALIAN, RUSSIAN...
– AMERICAN.
AMERICAN?!
ALSO KNOWN AS KETCHUP TO THE UNINITIATED.
MACNELLY

THREE BEERS?
SURE.
SAY, SINCE THERE ARE THREE OF US, WHY DON'T WE GET A PITCHER?
OKAY...
THREE PITCHERS.
MACNELLY

ROZ!...BEER ALL AROUND!!

MACNELLY

8

HOW MUCH HAVE YOU LOST AT THAT WEIGHT-REDUCING CLINIC?
ABOUT 4 POUNDS.
BUT I LOST IT IN THE WORST PLACE.
MY WALLET.
MACNELLY

BY JEFF MACNELLY
MENU?
THANKS.

HEY, MUFFY... IS THAT A NEW SWEATER?
YES, ROZ...!! DON'T YOU THINK IT'S DIVINE?!!

I ORDERED IT FROM L.L. BEAK.
SEE... HERE'S THEIR CATALOGUE.

LOOK AT ALL THE COLORS THIS SWEATER COMES IN...

9

WINE... BURGUNDY... BRANDY...

CHAMPAGNE...

HEY! I'LL HAVE WHAT'S SHE'S HAVING!!
MACNELLY

10

JUST ONE SANDWICH, PERFESSER?... I'M PROUD OF YOU...

I OVEREAT ONLY WHEN I'M WORRIED ABOUT SOMETHING.

THAT'S GOOD, BECAUSE OVEREATING LEADS TO FAT BUILD-UP, WHICH CAN CAUSE SERIOUS CARDIO-VASCULAR PROBLEMS.

GIMME FOUR GRILLED CHEESE.

MACNELLY.

I'LL HAVE THE WAIST-WATCHER MINI-SALAD.
WHAT DO YOU WANT ON THAT?
THREE SCOOPS OF CHOCOLATE CHIP, AND SOME MARSHMALLOW SAUCE.
MACNELLY

ROZ, THAT'S THE BEST FISH I EVER PUT IN MY MOUTH!
REALLY?
IT TASTED JUST LIKE CHICKEN!
MACNELLY

SHOE
BY MACNELLY
HI, PERFESSER! YOU'RE LOOKING MIGHTY SPIFFY!

GEEZ, PUT ON A CLEAN SHIRT AND WOMEN GO CRAZY.

Y'KNOW, SHOE, I THINK THE PERFESSER IS CLEANING UP HIS ACT.

LOOK, HE'S EVEN GOT A SILK HANDKERCHIEF THAT MATCHES HIS TIE.

FOR HIM, THAT'S GETTING DOWNRIGHT DAPPER!

SCHWONK!

HEY, THAT'S A NICE HANDKERCHIEF YOU GOT THERE, PERFESSER.

WHAT HANDKERCHIEF?
MACNELLY

YOU'RE EATING TOO MUCH, PERFESSER...YOU REALLY HAVE TO EXERCISE MORE.
I DO... I DO. IN FACT I WALKED ALL THE WAY OVER HERE FOR LUNCH...

I HAD TO WALK OFF BREAKFAST, ACTUALLY.

ROZ, DO CUSTOMERS REALLY FILL IN THESE SUGGESTION CARDS?
ALL THE TIME... LOOK IN THE BOX.
HERE'S ONE...
IT SAYS, "BETTER THAN YOUR TOAST."
MACNELLY

WHO'S THAT?
YOT.
HIS NAME IS YOT?
THAT'S WHAT I CALL HIM...
IT'S SHORT FOR "YOU OVER THERE."
MACNELLY

14

OUR VEGETARIAN DISH OF THE DAY IS "SURF AND TURF."
A VEGETARIAN "SURF AND TURF"?!

IT'S A BOWL OF MUDDY SEAWEED.
MACNELLY

SHOE
BY JEFF MACNELLY

SPAGHETTI, CHOCOLATE MALT, FRIED O. RINGS...
NOT SO FAST, GUYS.
MENU ROZ'S ROOST
MENU ROZ'S ROOST

HEY, ROZ, WHAT'S THE DEAL HERE?... YOU CHANGED THE MENU!
GEEZ...IS ANY OF THIS STUFF EDIBLE?

YUP... I'VE CHANGED THE MENU.

—FOR YOUR OWN GOOD.

NOW I USE ALL NATURAL INGREDIENTS...
ORGANICALLY GROWN WITH NO PRESERVATIVES.

BUT WITH MY INNOVATIVE RECIPES YOU WON'T BE ABLE TO TELL THE DIFFERENCE,

AND THINK OF HOW MUCH BETTER IT IS FOR YOU!
MACNELLY

OKAY... SO WHO'S FIRST?
I GUESS I'LL HAFTA GO WITH THE SUNFLOWER SEED PARMIGIANA.
MAKE IT TWO.

ROZ, COULD I SEE YOUR NEWSPAPER?...
SURE.
ARE YOU THROUGH WITH IT?
OH YEAH.
ARE YOU THROUGH WITH THIS?
MACNELLY

YUP. FIRST THING EVERY MORNING I GET THE OLD CARDIO-VASCULAR SYSTEM PUMPING IN HIGH GEAR...
AEROBIC DANCING?...
NOT EXACTLY...
I READ YOUR EDITORIAL PAGE.
PRESS
MACNELLY

MEXICAN FOOD IS CONFUSING.
I DON'T KNOW WHETHER I SHOULD EAT IT HERE, OR TAKE IT HOME...
AND CAULK MY TUB.
MACNELLY

NAH, I DON'T USUALLY FIX MY OWN MEALS...
I HATE COOKING AT HOME.
I DON'T SEE WHY... IT WOULD GIVE YOU A NICE CHANGE OF PACE...
FROM WHATEVER IT IS YOU DO AROUND HERE.
MACNELLY

SHOE
BY JEFF MACNELLY
WHAT'LL IT BE, BOYS?...
HMMM... I DON'T KNOW...

WHAT'S THAT DUDE DRINKING?

WHOA NOW!! CATCH THOSE TWO SPACE CADETS THERE..
I BELIEVE THOSE ARE SPECIMENS OF THE PUNK ROCK VARIETY...

WELL, THEY OUGHTA CRAWL BACK UNDER THEIR ROCK...

DO YOU THINK THEY COULD EVER GET A JOB LOOKING LIKE THAT?..
SURE... MAYBE IN THE MOVIES...
IF THEY EVER DO "WEST SIDE STORY" ON SATURN... HAR HAAAR!!
HA HAAA HAA HOHO!!
HOHOHOHO AHEE HAW HAR HAR

WILL YOU CLOWNS KNOCK IT OFF?

THOSE TWO HAPPEN TO BE REGULAR CUSTOMERS OF MINE! THEY DON'T CAUSE ANY TROUBLE, AND THEY ARE WELCOME IN MY RESTAURANT!!
IT'S A FREE COUNTRY!!

BESIDES, THEY SCARE OFF THE COCKROACHES...
MACNELLY.

I'M THINKING OF ADDING A NEW ROOM ONTO THE ROOST HERE...
GEE, THAT'S GONNA COST A BUNCH.
NO SWEAT... I CAN SWING IT.
WHERE ARE YOU GONNA FIND THAT KIND OF MONEY?
I'LL GET YOU TO PAY YOUR BAR TAB...
MACNELLY

THERE'S NOTHING TO FEAR ABOUT GETTING OLD...
I MEAN, AGING IS JUST A STATE OF FLORIDA...
YOU MEAN "MIND"... "STATE OF MIND."
WHATEVER.
MACNELLY

WELL, HOW DID YOU LIKE THE CHILI?
VERY VERSATILE, ROZ...
VERSATILE?! WHAT DOES THAT MEAN?!!
WELL, IF YOU CAN'T EAT IT, YOU CAN ALWAYS USE IT TO UNCLOG YOUR DRAINS.
MACNELLY

GIMME A LARGE PEPPERONI PIZZA...
YOU WANT THAT THIN AND CRUSTY,
OR THICK AND CHEWY?
JUST MAKE IT HOT AND MASSIVE.
MACNELLY

SHOE
BY JEFF MACNELLY
LAST CALL, GENTLEMEN!

YOU TOO, PERFESSER.

ANOTHER BEER, MAN MOUNTAIN?
SURE, ROZ, THANKS...
BOY, THIS JOGGING REALLY TAKES IT OUT OF YOU.
A FEW BREWS HELP MAKE A PHYSICAL FITNESS PROGRAM BEARABLE.

WELL, I BETTER START THINKING ABOUT TAKING OFF...

GOSH, IT'S ALMOST MIDNIGHT!!

SEE YA, ROZ...
I DON'T WANT TO TURN INTO A PUMPKIN...
OH NO!
TOO LATE!
MACNELLY

PERFESSER? ARE YOU OKAY?
UH, YEAH, ROZ I THINK SO.

I BELIEVE I'VE BEEN OVERSERVED AGAIN.
MACNELLY

DO YOU TAKE AMERICAN EXPRESS?
NO, SORRY...

ONLY MAJOR GAS CREDIT CARDS.
MACNELLY

WHAT'LL IT BE, PERFESSER?
GEE, I DON'T KNOW, ROZ...
IT'S BEEN SUCH A ROUGH DAY...
I GUESS I'LL HAVE WHAT THE GENTLEMAN ON THE FLOOR IS HAVING.
MACNELLY

I DON'T SEE HOW YOU CAN GAG DOWN THAT COFFEE.
I LOVE IT!
COFFEE IS LIKE HAVING DESSERT AFTER BREAKFAST.
OF COURSE, IF YOU HAVE A CIGAR FOR BREAKFAST, ANYTHING TASTES GREAT.
MACNELLY

Shoe®
BY JEFF MACNELLY
I FINALLY GOT ONE OF THOSE FANCY FOOD PROCESSORS...
YEAH, I'VE HAD ONE FOR YEARS...

IT'S CORDLESS.

I THINK I'LL CHECK OUT MY NEW FOOD PROCESSOR...
HMMM... "IMPORTANT DIRECTIONS"...
"SAFETY TIPS"...

HECK, LET'S SEE HOW YOU CUT THIS SUCKER ON...

♫
CLICK CLICK...

RRRR

"SAFETY TIP NO. 6: DO NOT OPERATE WHILE WEARING A NECKTIE..."
MACNELLY

THIS CEREAL IS AWFUL!!
BUT IT'S GOOD FOR YOU - IT'S HIGH IN NATURAL FIBER.
IF I WANTED NATURAL FIBER FOR BREAKFAST I'D FRY UP MY DOORMAT...
MACNELLY

PERFESSER,... I THOUGHT YOU WERE WATCHING YOUR WAISTLINE.
NOPE.
NOT ANYMORE, ROZ.
HOW CAN YOU WATCH SOMETHING YOU CAN'T SEE?
MACNELLY

Y'KNOW I'M GETTING SO FORGETFUL LATELY...
SOMETIMES I THINK I'M LOSING MY... UH..
WHATCHACALLIT...
MACNELLY.

26

I ALWAYS HAVE MIXED FEELINGS ABOUT SEEING A MAGNIFICENT SUNSET LIKE THIS FROM ATOP ONE OF YOUR BARSTOOLS, ROZ...
BECAUSE IT MEANS HAPPY HOUR IS ALMOST OVER...
NOT THIS TIME, PERFESSER...
THAT'S A SUNRISE..
MACNELLY

Shoe
BY MACNELLY
I THINK I'LL HAVE A LITTLE DINNER...
ROZ'S Menu

TO TIDE ME OVER 'TIL MY MIDNIGHT SNACK.
ROZ'S Menu

ROZ'S ROOST
WHAT'LL IT BE, "TONS-OF-FUN"?
WELL, THIS CHEESE CAKE LOOKS GOOD.
ROZ'S Menu

AND AN ORDER OF FRENCH FRIES... A PITCHER OF BEER...
ROZ'S Menu

A COFFEE MILKSHAKE, AND A SLICE OF THAT CHOCOLATE CREAM PIE.
ROZ'S Menu

THAT IS THE UNHEALTHIEST EXCUSE FOR A DINNER THAT I HAVE EVER HEARD...
ROZ'S MENU

WHAT ABOUT YOUR VITAMINS?...YOU GOTTA HAVE YOUR GREENS...
OKAY, OKAY...

GIMME A DISH OF MINT CHOCOLATE CHIP.
MACNELLY

I'VE REALLY GOT TO STOP SMOKING...
OH BROTHER...
I THINK THE WAY TO DO IT IS TO CUT DOWN GRADUALLY... TOMORROW I'LL SMOKE FIVE FEWER CIGARETTES THAN I SMOKED TODAY.
HOW WILL YOU DO THAT?
I'LL WAKE UP TEN MINUTES LATER.
MACNELLY.

WE ALL HAVE BUG PROBLEMS SOMETIMES...
BUT THIS IS GETTING SERIOUS.
MY ROACH MOTEL IS GOING CONDO.
MACNELLY

YECCH!! THIS ★#@?!! COFFEE!!
WHAT'S THE MATTER? IT'S CINNAMON CAFÉ AU LAIT À LA MODE. IT'S DELICIOUS!!
– I KNOW.
COFFEE'S NOT SUPPOSED TO TASTE GOOD.
MACNELLY

SHOE
BY MACNELLY
THANKS, ROZ... THAT WAS GREAT...
ROZ'S ROOST

WHAT WAS IT?

GAK! THESE SPOTS ON THE BACK OF MY HAND!
AGE SPOTS!! I NEVER NOTICED THEM BEFORE!
IT'S JUST ANOTHER SIGN THAT I'M AGING...

I'M DETERIORATING BEFORE MY EYES! AND THERE'S NOTHING I CAN DO ABOUT IT!!

OH, COME ON, PERFESSER, EVERYBODY GROWS OLD. DON'T WORRY ABOUT IT.

AND, ANYWAY, THOSE AREN'T AGE SPOTS ON YOUR HAND...

THAT'S WHERE YOU DROOLED YOUR CHILI.
MACNELLY

WHAT IS THAT GOOEY STUFF?
I DON'T HAVE THE SLIGHTEST IDEA.
I'M SURE IT'S FANTASTIC, THOUGH.
ALL STICKY FOOD IS GREAT FOOD.
MACNELLY

Y'KNOW, BECAUSE THIS PLACE IS SUCH A HANGOUT FOR ALL OF YOU NEWSPAPER GUYS IT'S GOTTEN QUITE A REPUTATION.
IN FACT, IT'S BEING WRITTEN UP IN AN INTERNATIONAL PUBLICATION.
YOU MEAN THE MICHELIN GUIDE OR SOMETHING?
NO, THE GUINNESS BOOK OF WORLD RECORDS — UNDER "LOWEST TIPPING."
MACNELLY

OKAY IF I GIVE THIS LEFTOVER MEATLOAF TO THE DOG, ROZ?
SURE.
HERE, BOY!!
I KNOW YOU CAN'T CHEW IT... JUST DO US ALL A BIG FAVOR AND BURY IT, WILLYA?
MACNELLY

WANT ANY MORE?
NO THANKS.
I'M JUST GONNA FEED IT TO THE DOG.
WELL, OKAY...
I HATE TO SEE SMALL ANIMALS SUFFER.
MACNELLY

Shoe®
By Jeff MacNelly
NO.

I SAID, TAKE A SWIG...

WHAT I'M ABOUT TO TELL YOU IS CRUCIAL TO THE GAME OF GOLF.

KEEP YOUR HEAD STEADY.

FIRM GRIP... BUT NOT TOO TIGHT.

THIS ELBOW... SLIGHTLY BENT.

33

REMEMBER YOUR FOLLOW-THROUGH.

NOW LET'S TRY IT.
MACNELLY

ROZ?

TWO MORE...

WATCH THAT MARTINI, PAL...
IT'LL HAVE YOU SEEING STARS...
OH, PISH.
GROG
THE BIG DIPPER,... ORION,... AND THERE'S POLARIS....
MACNELLY

34

PERFESSER! YOU'RE STICKING TO YOUR DIET!
IT'S EASY.
I FOLLOW THE FIRST RULE OF SUCCESSFUL DIETING...
"NEVER LET ANYONE SEE YOU EAT."
MACNELLY

YOU'VE GOT TO EAT BETTER, PERFESSER. YOUR BODY IS YOUR TEMPLE, YOU KNOW.
SURE.
MAYBE YOUR BODY IS A TEMPLE...
MINE'S A TOXIC WASTE DUMP.
MACNELLY

35

YOU'RE SMOKING AGAIN, ROZ.
I KNOW, I KNOW.
IT HELPS ME COPE WITH TRAUMATIC, STRESSFUL PERIODS IN MY LIFE.
LIKE WHEN I'M QUITTING SMOKING.
MACNELLY

Shoe
BY MACNELLY
AH, BREAKFAST! THE MOST IMPORTANT MEAL OF THE DAY.
Menu

-MORE IMPORTANT THAN ANY OF THE OTHER FIVE.
Menu

TODAY'S SPECIAL: Freshly Squeezed Orange Juice
MORNIN', PERFESSER.
IS THAT O.J. REALLY FRESH SQUOZE, ROZ?

YUP. SQUEEZED RIGHT BEFORE YOUR EYES.
Menu

PUT ME DOWN FOR A LARGE GLASS THEN...
COMIN' UP.

SQUEEZE SQUEEZE
FROZEN
BLOOP!
MACNELLY

ROZ, I HAVE A BONE TO PICK WITH YOU...

AND IT CAME FROM MY COFFEE...
MACNELLY

IT'S JUST NOT FAIR. A GARBAGEMAN MAKES MORE THAN A WOMAN BANKER IN CHICAGO!
THAT'S AN ISOLATED CASE....
OVERALL, WOMEN MAKE A LOT MORE THAN MEN.
OH, YEAH? HOW DO YOU FIGURE?
OVERALL, YOU LIVE LONGER.
MACNELLY.

GUACAMOLE?
NO THANKS.

I NEVER EAT ANYTHING THAT LOOKS LIKE SOMETHING I MAY HAVE STEPPED IN.
MACNELLY

38

YOU KNOW, SKYLER... WHEN I WAS YOUR AGE I WAS QUITE THE ATHLETE. ...QUICK, AGILE...
THEN HE DEVELOPED FURNITURE PROBLEMS...
FURNITURE PROBLEMS?
HIS CHEST FELL INTO HIS DRAWERS.
MACNELLY

SHOE
BY MACNELLY
ROZ'S ROOST
THERE GOES A 23!

ON A SCALE FROM 1 TO 10.

ROZ'S
OKAY, SHOE, ON A SCALE OF ONE TO TEN, WHERE DO I RATE?
WELL, ROZ... TO BE HONEST...

YOU RATE TEN -NO QUESTION.

ROZ'S ROOST
REALLY?
YUP.

39

ROZ'S ROOST
LEGS: 2
ARMS: 3
FACE: 4
PERSONALITY: 1...

THWACK!

THE TRUTH ALWAYS HURTS.
MACNELLY

EVERY TIME HE HAS THREE CUPS OF COFFEE IT TURNS HIM INTO A GROUCH...
I BETCHA IT'S ALL THAT CAFFEINE.... I MEAN, HAVE YOU EVER SEEN HIM DRINK ANYTHING ELSE THAT MADE HIM AS GRUMPY?...
YEAH... ONCE.
THE TIME HE HAD THREE CUPS OF YOUR DECAFFEINATED COFFEE.
MACNELLY

DO WE HAVE TO HAVE RESERVATIONS TO EAT HERE?
YOU REALLY SHOULD...

EVERYONE ELSE HAS RESERVATIONS ABOUT EATING HERE...
MACNELLY

WOW, ROZ, IT MUST BE REALLY EXCITING TO RUN THE OFFICIAL NEWSPAPER HANGOUT!
SURE IS.

ESPECIALLY IF YOU GET EXCITED BY CRANKY OLD GEEZERS WHO ARE ALLERGIC TO TIPPING...
MACNELLY

OKAY, I CAN ACCEPT LIGHT BEER, I GUESS...

BUT SALT-FREE PRETZELS...
THEY'RE PART OF A COMMUNIST PLOT.
MACNELLY

Shoe®
By Jeff MacNelly
All you can eat $9.95

OR, "ALL YOU CAN STOMACH."

I'LL HAVE A SALAD.
HELP YOURSELF TO OUR SALAD BAR.

OKAY... AND I'LL HAVE THE FETTUCINI...

THERE'S OUR PASTA BAR. HELP YOURSELF WHEN YOU'RE READY.

AND I THINK I'LL HAVE SOME DESSERT.
SURE.

HELP YOURSELF TO OUR SUNDAE BAR.

HEY, ROZ...
SHOULD I ASK FOR THE CHECK ...

OR SHOULD I JUST HELP MYSELF TO THE CASH BAR?
MACNELLY

LOOK AT THE ROLE MODELS THE KIDS OF TODAY HAVE...
FREAKY ROCK SINGERS, OVERPAID BALLPLAYERS, SLEAZY POLITICIANS !!... SO UNLIKE OUR HEROES WHEN WE WERE KIDS.
RIGHT. MY HERO NEVER TOOK DRUGS OR GOT INTO TROUBLE. NO, SIR...
..MR. POTATO HEAD NEVER LET ME DOWN.
MACNELLY

WITH THIS SIMPLE GRIP EXERCISER YOU CAN LOSE 25 POUNDS IN ONE WEEK.
YOU MEAN BY JUST SQUEEZING THIS THING...
NO, DUMMY, LIKE THIS:
MACNELLY.

I'M REALLY IN TROUBLE... I LOST A REAL BUNDLE AT THE TRACK...
THAT DOESN'T SURPRISE ME...
YOU COULDN'T MAKE IT A WEEK WITHOUT GAMBLING.
WANNA BET?
MACNELLY

I'LL HAVE THE DIET SALAD...
YOU WANT THE DIET DRESSING?
SURE... WHAT IS IT?
500 ISLAND.
MACNELLY

SHOE®
By Jeff MacNelly
YOU DONE WITH THE PAPER, ROZ?
SURE..

BUT THE FISH ISN'T.

LET'S SEE... VIRGO ...HERE IT IS:

"You should watch what you eat.

You're not fat. If anything, you look a little peaked.

You work too hard...

You're just like your father.

Is that a new tie?

You got the one I sent you, I hope...

Call your sister. She listens to you."
HEY! WHAT KIND OF HOROSCOPE IS THIS?

IT'S A NEW FEATURE:

"Your Mommoscope."
MacNelly

WHAT ARE YOU UP TO NOW?

I KNOW I HAVE A BOOK IN ME...

AND IF YOU'RE SMART YOU'LL LEAVE IT THERE.
MACNELLY

46

I THINK WE'VE REACHED A PLATEAU IN THIS HIGH-TECH REVOLUTION...

HOW DO YOU MEAN?

I'M STARTING TO GET COMPUTERIZED PHONE MESSAGES ON MY MACHINE.
MACNELLY

I'LL NEVER LOSE ANY WEIGHT.
SURE YOU WILL! JUST USE SOME COMMON SENSE.
THE BEST RULE OF THUMB FOR A SENSIBLE DIET...
IS "NEVER EAT ANYTHING BIGGER THAN YOUR HEAD."
MACNELLY

A BIRTHDAY CAKE!! FOR ME??...
HAPPY BIRTHDAY, PERFESSER!!
CAN I LIGHT THE CANDLES?
NOT YET, SKYLER.
WAIT FOR THE FIRE MARSHAL.
MACNELLY

I FIGURED IT OUT, ROZ.
WHAT?
I GAIN WEIGHT BECAUSE I HAVE ALL THAT TIME BETWEEN MEALS TO SNACK.
GOOD. SO YOU'RE CUTTING DOWN ON ALL THAT EATING BETWEEN MEALS?
NO. I'M CUTTING DOWN ON ALL THAT TIME BETWEEN MEALS.
MACNELLY

THAT WAS ABSOLUTELY DELICIOUS!!
I SIMPLY MUST HAVE THE RECIPE!
RIGHT. "TAKE 400 THOUSAND HEAD OF CATTLE..."
MACNELLY.

WOW! EIGHT BIG TURNOVERS FOR THE COWBOYS!!
WHAT'S SO GREAT ABOUT THAT?
HE'S HAD TWELVE ALREADY...
AND WE'RE NOT IN THE FOURTH QUARTER.
URP

WHAT'S THE SPECIAL?
"POTLUCK."
WHAT DOES LUCK HAVE TO DO WITH IT?
YOU'RE LUCKY IF YOU MAKE IT TO THE NEXT MEAL.

HER? ARE YOU KIDDING? I DON'T KNOW WHAT YOU SEE IN HER...

I'M NOT SURE MYSELF...

I THINK IT'S A CERTAIN CHEMISTRY...

YEAH ... ALCOHOL AND GERITOL.

MACNELLY

Shoe
By Jeff MacNelly

HOW DO YOU TELL IF THIS IS "GOOD" CHOLESTEROL OR "BAD" CHOLESTEROL?
TAKE A BITE.

IF IT TASTES REAL GOOD, IT'S BAD CHOLESTEROL.

YOU'VE LOST WEIGHT.

I HAVE?
SURE.

I COULD TELL AS SOON AS YOU WALKED IN...
MACNELLY

I DON'T FEEL SKINNIER.
NOT YOUR FACE.

IT'S MOSTLY YOUR CABOOSE...

YOUR REAR END.

OH THAT... YEAH, I DID DROP A FEW POUNDS THERE.

I CLEANED OUT MY WALLET.

IS IT "STARVE A COLD, FEED A FEVER," OR THE OTHER WAY AROUND?
WHY, WHAT DO YOU HAVE?

YOU MUST BE RACKING UP A WHOLE BUNCH OF FREQUENT FLYER MILES...
YEAH.
BUT AFTER ALL THE FLYING I'VE DONE THIS PAST YEAR...

I WISH THEY'D GIVE ME A TRAIN TICKET.
MACNELLY

YES, SKYLER, TONIGHT IS SEAFOOD NIGHT...
..BUT I'VE GOT NEWS FOR YOU.
SALTWATER TAFFY IS NOT A SEAFOOD.
MACNELLY

SHOE
By Jeff MacNelly
THIS IS GREAT COFFEE!

EITHER THAT, OR IT'S REAL BAD ONION SOUP...

YOU FINISHED HERE?
YEAH. THANKS.

GOOD GRIEF!!
VOOMP

DO YOU ALWAYS HAVE TO DO THAT?

AS SOON AS YOU PUT DOWN YOUR FORK, YOU FIRE UP ONE OF THOSE GROSS STOGIES...

YOU MEN ALWAYS HAVE TO STICK SOMETHING IN YOUR MOUTH AFTER DINNER...

— IF IT'S NOT A STINKING CIGAR, IT'S A TOOTHPICK.

IS IT LIKE A PACIFIER OR SOMETHING?...
NO, NOT REALLY...

IT'S JUST THAT AFTER A MEAL LIKE THAT ONE...

THIS CIGAR IS AN AFTER-DINNER MINT.

WHAT'S THIS?
IT'S OUR HOUSE WINE — VERY NICE... WITH A VERY EXCITING FINISH.
WHAT THE HECK DOES THAT MEAN?
FINISH THE BOTTLE AND YOU'LL SEE...
MACNELLY

DO YOU THINK THESE BIG FIGHTS ARE FIXED?
IT'S HARD TO SAY.

BUT DO YOU THINK THE WORDS "HONEST" AND "SIX-MILLION-DOLLAR PAYDAY"...
EVER APPEAR IN THE SAME SENTENCE?
MACNELLY

NOW THAT OAT BRAN IS OUT, WHERE AM I GOING TO GET MY HIGH-FIBER BREAKFAST?
NO PROBLEM FOR ME.
I JUST CHEW MY CIGAR INSTEAD OF SMOKING IT.
MACNELLY

I'LL HAVE THE OYSTERS, THE CAESAR SALAD... THE CHICKEN BREAST,
THE LINGUNI WITH CLAM SAUCE, THE SEA SCALLOPS...
AND THE VEAL PARMIGIANA.
ON WHOLE WHEAT.
MACNELLY

Shoe®
By Jeff MacNelly
PARDON ME, SIR... COULD I BUY YOUR COMPANY FOR, SAY, 162 MILLION...?
I'M SORRY..

@!?*# VENTURE CAPITALIST..

SO, WHAT DO YOU DO FOR A LIVING?
I'M A COMMODITIES TRADER.
REALLY?...YOU'RE ONE OF THOSE GUYS WHO YELL AND SCREAM AT EACH OTHER IN A BIG PIT WHILE YOU SWAP HOG BELLIES AND PLYWOOD?...
WELL, SORT OF.

GOSH, I NEVER UNDERSTOOD HOW THAT WORKS. IT ALL LOOKS SO INSANE.
IT'S NOT AS PRIMITIVE AS THAT...

WE DON'T ACTUALLY LUG AROUND SLABS OF BACON – IT'S A LOT MORE SOPHISTICATED THAN THAT.

57

THE ADVANCES IN COMPUTER TECHNOLOGY HAVE ACTUALLY STREAMLINED THE BUSINESS OF TRADING COMMODITIES.

NOWADAYS, WE CAN SIMPLY BYPASS THE PAPERWORK AND THE MIDDLEMEN...
..SO WE CAN CONCENTRATE ON THE NERVE CENTER OF OUR CAPITALIST SYSTEM:

MERCEDES FUTURES.
MACNELLY

I'VE DECIDED TO GO INTO CATERING ON THE SIDE.
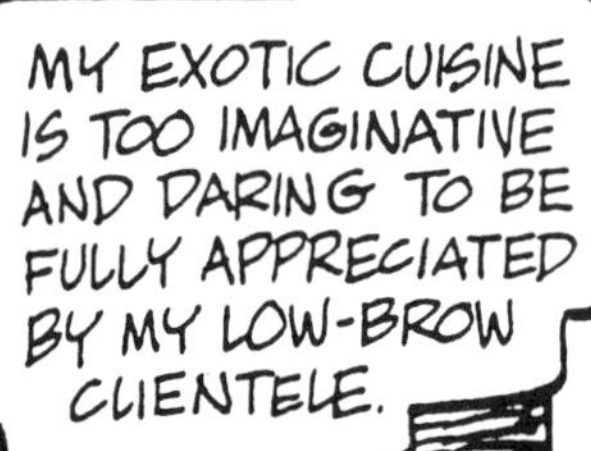
MY EXOTIC CUISINE IS TOO IMAGINATIVE AND DARING TO BE FULLY APPRECIATED BY MY LOW-BROW CLIENTELE.

YOU GOT A NAME FOR THIS VENTURE?

HOW 'BOUT "EELS ON WHEELS"?

58

YEAH, I KNOW I ALWAYS WEAR THE SAME STUFF. SO WHAT?
WELL, WOULDN'T YOU LIKE TO MAKE YOUR OWN FASHION STATEMENT?

NOPE. I JUST LIKE TO MAKE A FASHION QUESTION:

"HOW MUCH?"

CAN I HELP YOU?
I'M HERE TO COLLECT THE PERRIER WE HAD TO RECALL.
BOY, DID YOU COME TO THE WRONG JOINT!...

"A WOMAN IS ONLY A WOMAN,
BUT A GOOD CIGAR...
IS A NO-PEST STRIP FOR WOMEN..."

Shoe®
By Jeff MacNelly
PSST! WANT SOME HOT INSIDE INFORMATION?
GREAT! WHERE'S THE BEST PLACE TO PUT MY SAVINGS?

INSIDE THIS JAR.

IT'S GETTING HARDER AND HARDER FOR ALL US LITTLE GUYS TO FIND A GOOD, SAFE PLACE TO PUT OUR MONEY.
RIGHT.

THE BIG BOYS AND THE HIGH ROLLERS GET ALL THAT INSIDER INFORMATION...

THEY DON'T HAVE TO WORRY AS MUCH AS THE REST OF US...

THEY HAVE THE CONTACTS, THE HOT TIPS,
AND THE MONEY.

IN THE END, I GUESS YOU JUST HAVE TO GET OPINIONS FROM PEOPLE YOU TRUST — AND GO WITH YOUR GUT.

...DO YOU THINK THIS IS A DECENT INVESTMENT, IRV?
HMM...

YEAH, YOU CAN'T GO WRONG WITH THAT ONE...

BUT ORDER IT WITH THE STEAK FRIES.
MacNelly

BOY, YOU THINK YOU'VE PLANNED FOR EVERYTHING, AND THEN —ZAP!— TRAGEDY STRIKES...
WHAT HAPPENED?

MY INSURANCE COMPANY JUST PASSED AWAY.

JUST A SECOND, MAC! AREN'T YOU FORGETTING SOMETHING?...
AH, YES...

THE TIP.
MACNELLY

WHAT SHOULD I HAVE TO DRINK TONIGHT, ROZ?
BEATS ME...

WHAT ILLUSION ARE YOU TRYIN' TO ACHIEVE?

62

BUT I LIKED YOUR EX-WIFE...

SHE HAD A GOOD HEART...
I KNOW.

IT JUST WASN'T PUMPING ENOUGH BLOOD TO HER BRAIN...

Shoe
By Jeff MacNelly
WILL YOU BE HAVING WINE WITH YOUR DINNER, SIR?
WHY, YES...

WHAT GOES GOOD WITH A SIX-PACK?
WINE LIST

MORE WINE, PERFESSER?

NO, THANKS. THIS IS FINE.
BUT I THINK I NEED TO ASK YOU FOR YOUR KEYS...
WHAT?

HEY, I HAVEN'T BEEN DRINKING... —YOU HAVE!
ONLY HALF A GLASS.

COME ON... LET'S HAVE THE KEYS.
BUT THIS IS CRAZY!!

LISTEN, ROZ, I'M YOUR FRIEND...
OKAY, OKAY... BUT I DON'T SEE WHY YOU WANT MY CAR KEYS...

NOT YOUR CAR KEYS...

THE KEYS TO YOUR WINE CELLAR...

THIS STUFF SHOULD BE LOCKED UP BEFORE IT HURTS SOMEBODY.

SOMETHING TO TAKE YOUR MIND OFF YOUR TROUBLES?
NO, ROZ, SOMETHING STRONGER.
SOMETHING TO TAKE MY MIND OFF MY MIND.
MACNELLY

OKAY. I GOT A LIFE.

NOW WHAT?
MACNELLY

2 EGGS. OVER EASY. BACON.
HASH. GRITS.
HOMEFRIES. LARGE O. J.
CHEESE DANISH.
NAP.

WELL, I FINALLY ELIMINATED SOME MAJOR MONTHLY EXPENSES...
YUP! NO MORE CAR PAYMENTS FOR ME!
HOW'D YOU DO THAT?
I TOTALLED IT OVER THE WEEKEND.

Shoe
By Jeff MacNelly
I NEED SOME GOOD STUFF FOR THE GOSSIP COLUMN...

Things were hopping in Treetops over the weekend.
We saw many a bleary eye Saturday at the Kiwanis Pancake breakfast...

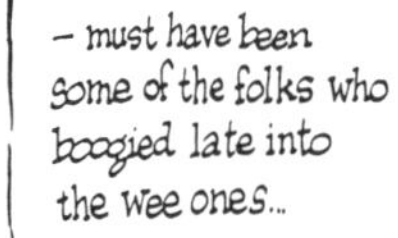
– must have been some of the folks who boogied late into the wee ones...

at Friday night's shindig at the new Fire House –
Speaking of which ...

Who was that mysterious lady in the red dress we saw dancing with Cecil Blevitt?

THAT WAS MARVA BEEVAX FROM SEVEN CRAGS – AN OLD FRIEND OF CECIL'S LATE WIFE, NADINE –

SHE HAPPENED TO BE IN TOWN FOR THE COUNTY WALLET-MAKING FESTIVAL...

AT LEAST THAT'S WHAT SHE CLAIMS...

SOME TOWNS ARE JUST TOO SMALL FOR A GOSSIP COLUMN.
MACNELLY

I'LL MAKE YOU A DEAL:

I WON'T EAT OUT OF YOUR ASHTRAY,

–YOU DON'T SMOKE IN MY RESTAURANT.

ASK US ABOUT OUR CATERING

SO, HOW'S YOUR CATERING GOING?

DON'T ASK.

FRESH PEPPER?
NO THANKS.
HOW FRESH COULD IT BE, ANYWAY?..

YOU'D ONLY HAVE TO FILL THOSE THINGS ONCE A DECADE.

HEY!! THIS IS A NON-SMOKING RESTAURANT...
OH YEAH?
WELL, SOMEBODY BETTER TELL THE BLACKENED REDFISH.

Shoe
By Jeff MacNelly
THIS IS ONE STRANGE JUKEBOX... NONE OF THE CLASSICS.

LIKE THE FOUR TOPS, THE ISLEY BROTHERS, MARTHA AND THE VANDELLAS...

HEY, BUDDY! DO ME A FAVOR AND PLAY B-17.
OH NO YOU DON'T!

I'M NOT HAVING THAT NOISE AGAIN! REMEMBER WHAT HAPPENED THE LAST TIME...

I JUST NEED TO HEAR IT ONCE MORE... —FOR OLD TIME'S SAKE.

IT REMINDS ME OF A GIRL I KNEW IN WORLD WAR II.

COME ON, PAL... FOR A VETERAN?..

OKAY. B-17...

I'M GETTING RID OF THAT JUKEBOX.
AIN'T SHE A BEAUTY?
MACNELLY

SOMETHING TO START?

YES. THE PEACH COBBLER WITH TWO SCOOPS OF VANILLA...

YOU'RE HAVING DESSERT FIRST?

THIS WAY I DON'T MAKE SUCH A PIG OF MYSELF AT DINNER.

MACNELLY

70

NEITHER RAIN NOR SNOW NOR DARK OF NIGHT,

WILL STAY THIS COURIER FROM HIS APPOINTED ROUNDS.
IT'S STILL POURING OUT THERE.
TATTLER
Tribune

GREAT!! ANOTHER APPOINTED ROUND!!

HEY, ROZ, WHAT IS THIS "TEX-MEX" FOOD, ANYHOW?
IT'S GOT A TEXAS INFLUENCE...

SO IT'S JUST LIKE MEXICAN,

ONLY LOUDER.

BY MACNELLY
MORNIN', ROZ...

WHATCHA GOT IN THAT JAR, PERFESSER?

ROOST
ROZ, I HAVE HERE THE LATEST THING IN RAT POISON...

SEE, THE RATS ARE LURED BY THE AROMA...

THEN THEY GORGE THEMSELVES ON THIS GLOP.

PRETTY SOON THEY GET TERRIBLY THIRSTY, AND THEY HEAD OUTSIDE LOOKING FOR WATER.

AND SOON AFTER THAT, THEY KEEL OVER FROM ACUTE GASTROINTESTINAL TRAUMA.
THAT'S FANTASTIC ...WHAT'S IN IT?

YOUR CHILI.
MACNELLY

ROZ, I'VE DECIDED I'VE REACHED THAT POINT IN MY LIFE WHERE I MUST SEEK LIGHTENMENT.

DON'T YOU MEAN ENLIGHTENMENT?

NO, I MEAN I'VE GOT TO LOSE TEN POUNDS...

WE'RE HERE AT INTERNATIONALLY FAMOUS ROZ'S ROOST,

AND WE'VE SECRETLY REPLACED THE COFFEE SHE NORMALLY SERVES...

WITH THIS 20-WEIGHT TRANSMISSION FLUID.

AMAZING!! I CAN'T TELL THE DIFFERENCE!!

IT'S A LOCAL RED WINE.

HOW IS IT?

WELL, IT NEEDS TO BREATHE A LITTLE.

PREFERABLY IN THE PARKING LOT.
© 1991 Tribune Media Services, Inc.
All Rights Reserved
12-13

THIS'LL PUT HAIR ON YOUR CHEST...
I'VE OFTEN WONDERED ABOUT THAT.
HOW DOES THE HAIR GET FROM THE COFFEE TO THE CHEST?
12/27
© 1991 Tribune Media Services, Inc.
All Rights Reserved

SHOE
BY MACNELLY
THAT WAS DELICIOUS!
ROZ'S ROOST

MY COMPLIMENTS TO THE CHEF ..er... CHEFETTE.

LET'S GET GOIN', PERFESSER...
ROZ'S ROOST

WHAT DID YOU HAVE, SHOE?
I HAD THE NUMBER 6 WITH JUICE.

THAT'LL BE $2.85...
KACHING!

AND YOU HAD....WAIT!... LET ME GUESS...YOU HAD SCRAMBLED EGGS...UM... TOMATO JUICE, AND TOAST WITH GRAPE JELLY.
YEAH! THAT'S RIGHT!

ROZ, YOU'RE AMAZING!!

I WONDER HOW SHE ALWAYS REMEMBERS WHAT I ORDERED.
MACNELLY

HIT ME, ROZ...
NOT SO FAST. THIS IS A VERY NICE RED WINE...
IT SHOULD FIRST BE DECANTED INTO A LARGE-MOUTHED RECEPTACLE.
LIKE I SAID...
MACNELLY

CAN I GET YOU A DRINK WHILE YOU LOOK AT THE MENU?
NO, THANKS.
ALLOW ME TO REPHRASE THAT:
BEFORE YOU LOOK AT THIS MENU, YOU BETTER HAVE A DRINK.
$
MACNELLY

ARE YOU DOING A RESTAURANT REVIEW?
NEW MENU
NO. YOU JUST CHANGED THE MENU AFTER 14 YEARS...
THIS IS A NEWS STORY.
NEW MENU
MACNELLY

Shoe
THIS IS A GREAT INTERNATIONAL RESTAURANT: FINE FRENCH FOOD SERVED WITH GERMAN EFFICIENCY AND JAPANESE COURTESY...
le Menu

AT OPEC PRICES.
le Menu

OUI, MONSIEUR?
I GUESS I'LL HAVE... UM... THIS ONE HERE...
le Menu

"le Biftek au Gratin Garni..." OUI?
YEAH... RIGHT... AND THIS HERE...
le Menu

OUI, M'SIEUR... "les Pommes Frites à la Française"...
RIGHT...

May I suggest the "Mousse au Chocolat" for dessert?
YEAH... THAT SOUNDS GREAT.
le Menu

AND SOME "Perrier" TO DRINK?
SURE... WHAT THE HECK...

HEY STAN! GIMME A C-BURGER, ALL TH' WAY!... ORDER O' FRIES!... PIECE O' THAT CHOCKLIT CREAM, ... AN' A TWO CENTS PLAIN!
MACNELLY

LET'S DO LUNCH!
NO, THANKS...

I DON'T DO LUNCH.

I EAT IT.
MACNELLY

IS MY CHEESECAKE READY?
YUP.

BUT I HOPE YOU KNOW THAT IT HAS ABSOLUTELY NO FIBER IN IT...

WHAT IF I EAT THE BOX, TOO?
MACNELLY

YES, WE ALLOW SMOKING...

BUT NOT CIGARS.

THEN THINK OF THIS AS A VERY UGLY CIGARETTE.

YOU SHOULD THINK OF MY CIGAR AS YOUR FRIEND.
HOW'S THAT?

IT KEEPS YOU FROM GETTING CLOSE TO ME.

Shoe
BY MACNELLY
ROZ'S ROOST

COFFEE?
I'LL RISK IT...

OH, NO... I'VE GOT AN AWFUL RUN IN MY STOCKING...

ROZ'S ROOST
IT MUST LOOK TERRIBLE.
NAH.

YOU CAN'T EVEN NOTICE IT...

JUST LOOKS LIKE ANOTHER VARICOSE VEIN.

CLONG

SOME WOMEN ARE DETERMINED NOT TO BE CHEERED UP.
MACNELLY

I REGRET TO ANNOUNCE A CHANGE IN MY MARITAL STATUS.
SORRY TO HEAR THAT, IRV.

YES, MY STATUS HAS GONE FROM HUSBAND AND PROVIDER...

TO YES-MAN AND INDENTURED SERVANT.

I'LL HAVE THE MEAT LOAF...
OKAY.
YOU GET THREE VEGETABLES WITH THAT.
THREE POTATOES.

THAT CACTUS IS A NICE TOUCH.
ENJOY.

IT'S YOUR APPETIZER.

SOUTHWEST CUISINE HITS EAST VIRGINIA.
MACNELLY.

I'M A VEGETARIAN...
SURE! WE HAVE A WONDERFUL TOFU BURGER...

WELL I'M A VERY STRICT VEGETARIAN.

DO YOU HAVE ANY TOFU BROCCOLI?
MACNELLY.

Shoe
BY JEFF MACNELLY
NOTHIN' LIKE A GOOD CIGAR...

WHEN YOU NEED TO GET AWAY FROM PEOPLE...

NOW LOOK, ROZ... I'VE HAD A ROUGH DAY... I'M GONNA HAVE A BEER AND A SMOKE.
AND I DON'T WANNA LISTEN TO A LOT OF TRASH FROM YOU ABOUT MY CIGARS.
HEY, NO SWEAT.

I SENT AWAY FOR SOME SPECIAL AIR FRESHENER.
ROZ'S ROOST

-THEY'RE FLYING IT IN ANY MINUTE...
FLYING IT IN?!

VROOM!

YEAH, IT'S INDUSTRIAL STRENGTH.
MACNELLY

MIND IF I SMOKE?
YES.
BUT IT'S A MILD CIGAR...
NOW THERE'S AN OXYMORON.
MACNELLY

HEY!! CUT THAT OUT! NO CHESS IN HERE...
WHAT?
IT'S BAD FOR BUSINESS.
IF WORD GOT AROUND, SMART PEOPLE MIGHT START HANGING OUT IN HERE.
MACNELLY

HOW 'BOUT THEM CUBS?
UNH.
YOU MEN NEVER TALK ABOUT YOUR FEELINGS...

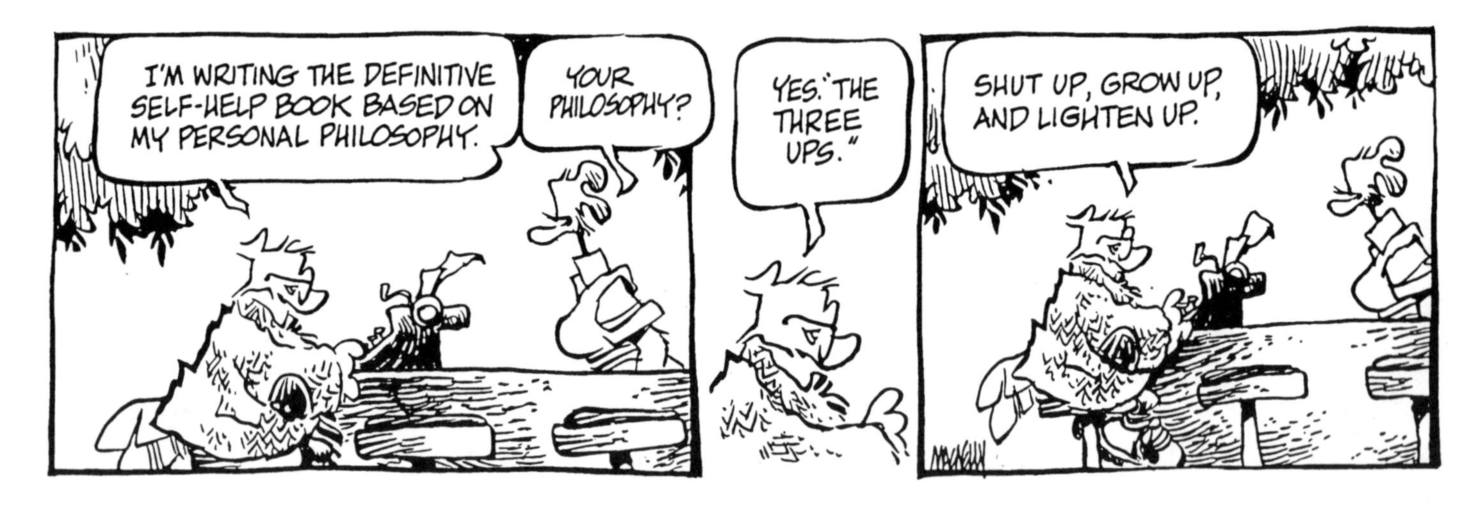

BY JEFF MACNELLY
COULD I HAVE SOME MORE, ROZ?

FINISH WHAT'S ON YOUR TIE FIRST.

I WISH YOU WOULD BE A LITTLE NEATER WHEN YOU EAT, PERFESSER.
IT'S A PAIN CLEANING UP AFTER YOU!!
YOU LEAVE CRUMBS ALL OVER THE COUNTER!

AND ON THE SEATS AND THE FLOOR.

THEN A LOT OF YOUR FOOD FALLS IN THE YARD...

AND THAT'S A REAL PROBLEM

IT ATTRACTS VARMINTS.
MACNELLY

WOULD YOU LIKE WINE WITH THAT?
WELL, LET'S SEE: RED MEAT—RED WINE, WHITE MEAT—WHITE WINE...

I'LL HAVE A GLASS OF GRAY.

AFTER-DINNER DRINK?

SURE... THE USUAL.

LISTERINE—NEAT!

BACON CHEESEBURGER, FRIES, CHOCOLATE SHAKE AND A SLAB OF THAT CHEESECAKE, PLEASE.

OKAY. IF IT'LL MAKE YOU FEEL BETTER, PUT IT ALL ON A HIGH-FIBER PLACEMAT.

LARGE PIZZA, EXTRA CHEESE, AND A CHOCOLATE SHAKE...

DON'T YOU EVER THINK ABOUT YOUR HEALTH?
YES.

TODAY I'M THINKING ABOUT MY MENTAL HEALTH.

WOULD YOU LIKE ME TO PUT THIS IN A WINE BUCKET FOR YOU?